ALAN RANGER

3.7 cm
Flak 18/36/37

STRATUS

Published in Poland in 2019
by Wydawnictwo Stratus sp.j.
Po. Box 123,
27-600 Sandomierz 1, Poland
e-mail: office@wydawnictwostratus.pl

as
MMPBooks
e-mail: office@mmpbooks.biz

www.mmpbooks.biz
www.wydawnictwostratus.pl

ISBN
978-83-65958-55-6

Editor in chief
Roger Wallsgrove

Editorial Team
Bartłomiej Belcarz
Robert Pęczkowski
Artur Juszczak

Cover
Dariusz Grzywacz

Book layout
Dariusz Grzywacz

DTP
Wydawnictwo Stratus sp.j.

PRINTED IN POLAND

Foreword

In this series of books, I have no intention of trying to add to what is already a very well docu – mented history of Germany's anti-aircraft defence systems and the associated Flak weaponry. It has been covered by many previous publications. Here I hope to give an impression, through original photographs taken both during and before war, of the 3.7 cm Flak guns and their crews as they dealt with the conditions in all the various theatres operation in which they found themselves.

Here in this publication I hope to show what was seen through the lens of the normal German soldier's camera, the soldiers that had to live with and operate these weapons each and every day, not the professional PK cameramen whose well-posed and sanitized shots are well known and have been published over and over again. As such they have been seen by most interested parties by now already. However the images taken by individual soldiers show a more personal view of the weapons and their installations in which the soldiers both lived and worked, the views that interested the common soldier not the professional propagandist. For the most part these photographs have been in private collections and have only recently come onto the market.

Most images we have used here were taken from prints made on old German Agfa paper stock, and the majority of these original prints are no more than 25 mm by 45 mm in size. Whilst we have used the best quality photos from my collection, occasionally, due to the interesting or the rare nature of the subject matter, a photo of a lesser quality has been included.

Introduction

The history of Germany's 3.7 cm Flak guns starts with the development of automatic-cannons by the Swiss manufacturer Solothurn, a wholly-owned subsidiary of the German armaments firm of Rheinmetall-Borsig, commonly known as just Rheinmetall. Solothurn was a company that Rheinmetall set up purely to circumvent the restrictions forced upon German military manufacturing by the terms of the 1919 Treaty of Versailles. The successful development of the 20 mm Solothurn Tankbuchse S18-1100 anti-aircraft cannon mount was in turn a development of Solothurn's S18-1000 20 mm semi-automatic anti-tank cannon, that was a world beater in the early 1930s. The two guns could even fire the same rounds and the 20-round magazine of the Flak 30 could easily be fitted to the S18-1000 20 mm semi-automatic anti-tank cannon, that was fitted with a 10-round magazine as standard.

Following the successful development of the Flak 30 anti-tank cannon, it was decided by Rheinmetail-Borsig & Solothurn to develop a larger calibre weapon upon the same design. This led to the 3.7 cm Flak 18 that was, as far as the actual gun is concerned, basically a scaled-up version of the 20 mm cannon. Its cradle and gun mount, however, were very different as they had both more weight to cope with as well as more extreme recoil forces.

The 3.7 cm Flak 18

The 3.7 cm anti-aircraft automatic cannon that was developed by Rheinmetall during 1934, and given the designation of the 3.7 cm Flak 18, had a 57 calibre barrel that was added to the weapon's full designation of 3.7 cm Flak 18 L/57. The gun was developed from the very start to be able to fire both anti-aircraft shrapnel burst and armour-piercing high explosive hollow point ammunition. It had the capability to fire up to a 4,800 m (15,700 ft) altitude with the anti-aircraft ammunition, and using the armour-piercing ammunition it could penetrate 36 mm of face-hardened cold-rolled armour plate placed at an incline of 60° from distance of 100 m. At a distance of 800 m it could penetrate 24 mm under the same test conditions, which at the time was better than many other nations' main anti-tank weaponry – if indeed. If indeed they even had specialized anti-tank weapons in their armoury in 1936, as many nations did not. The weapon had a practical rate of fire of 80 rounds per minute (RPM) and an all-up weight, including its transportation system, of 3,560 kg (7,850 lb) or 3.5 tonnes, whilst in its emplaced firing position configuration it weighed only 1,750 kg (3,860 lb) or 1.7 tonnes.

It became apparent very quickly, when the Flak 18 saw its combat service debut with the German Condor Legion in the Spanish Civil War (17th July 1936 until the 1st April 1939), that the weapon itself was be very effective once in firing position but was extremely unwieldy in its transportation configuration. It was slow to transition from its towed configuration to its firing configuration, and also in reverse, from ready to fire to ready to move. The cruciform mount and its associated twin-bogie system, the Sd. Anh. 104 that had been designed for it, (similar in design to the larger mounting used for the 88 mm Flak weapons), were both very heavy and extremely costly to manufacture. A redesign of the gun cradle, its base, as well as the mobility system, was begun as early as the winter of 1936. Thus the production of the Flak 18 was curtailed, as production was halted with all outstanding orders being placed on hold until the redesigned 3.7 cm Flak 36 became available to replace it.

The 3.7 cm Flak 18 was originally fitted to the anti-aircraft defence half-track variant of the Sd.Kfz. 6.5ton half-track the Sd.Kfz. 6/11[1], but was replaced during that vehicle's production run by the 3.7 cm Flak 36 as it became available.

The 3.7 cm Flak 36/37

The redesigned 3.7 cm Flak became known as the 3.7 cm Flak 36 L/57. Its ballistic properties were unchanged from the Flak 18 as it was essentially the same gun. However, due to the introduction of an ammunition loading tray attached to the gun cradle, the practical rate of fire rose to 120 RPM. Both the gun cradle and its associated transportation system were radically changed. The design was based upon a scaled-up version of the 2 cm Flak 30 design, resulting in a simplified and much lighter gun cradle and gun mount in the form of a gun table with a three point ground levelling pad arrangement and a two-wheeled trailer "U" shaped transportation system that had a hook at the end of the "U" that located into lugs on the gun mount's base plate. This was then was winched up to lock into the trailer by a winch mounted at the apex of the "U" where the towing mount was also located. This trailer was given the designation Sd. Anh. 52, that was also subsequently utilized as the trailer for the 2 cm *Flakvierling*. This revised design cost less to manufacture, used less material and weighed much less than its predecessor. In transportation mode it weighed 2,400 kg (3,420 lb) and in emplaced to fire position its weight was now only 1,550 kg (3,420 lb). With the introduction in late 1937 of an electrically operated sighting system mounted to the gun cradle, the Flakvisier 40 ranging computer replacing the originally supplied clockwork sight, the designation of the weapon was again changed to the 3.7 cm Flak 37 L57.

The Flak 36/37 was the most numerous variant of the 3.7 cm anti-aircraft gun and was produced in far larger numbers than any other variant, partly due to it also being produced under licence in Romania by the Astra company of Brasov. It was known in Romanian service as the Tun antiaerian Rheinmetall calibre 3.7 cm model 1939 and was manufactured at an average rate of 10 per month, but this fell as the was progressed.

The Flak 36/37 was commonly used on motorized chassis and featured as previously mentioned on the Sd.Kfz. 6/1. It was also fitted on the more numerous Sd.Kfz. 7/2 8-ton half-track as its mobile Flak variant of the standard Sd.Kfz. 7 artillery tractor. The weapon was also fitted onto the prototype of the 2 cm *Flakvierling auf Fahrgestell Panzerkampfwagen* IV *Möbelwagen* and ultimately fitted to the *Ostwind* anti-aircraft tank, also based on the Panzer IV hull, with the Flak 36/37 mounted in a specially designed turret.

---

1. More in the book Sd.Kfz. 6 *Mittlerer Zugkraftwagen 5t*, Camera ON 01, ISBN: 978-83-65281-70-8.

The 3.7 cm Flak 43

The last major production variant of the 3.7 cm Flak gun was the 3.7 cm Flak 43. It was a product born of the German need to reduce the amount of raw materials in all forms of military equipment production. It resulted from a major redesign of the 3.7 cm Flak 36/37 in order to save as much material as possible. Many of the weapon's cast and machined components were replaced with much lighter stamped or forged components. This major redesign also incorporated much of the newer technology developed by Rheinmetall in the development of their 30 mm MK 103 aircraft-mounted weapon system. The most significant change was the introduction of a gas-operated breech system that raised the practical rate of fire to 150 RPM. The weapon's emplaced weight was reduced to only 1,219 kg (2,687 lb). The redesigned weapon system still used the Sd. Anh. 52 trailer, but this too had undergone a slight redesign to both simplify production and use less precious steel in its manufacture.

Lastly, a *Flakzwilling* "twin" gun carriage was developed to mount two Flak 43s, one above the other. Whilst this twin mount did enter service it was only in very small numbers in the last few months of the war, and was not held in high regard by its crews. It was ungainly and difficult to operate and was also too heavy to be mounted on any existing standard flak-carrying vehicle without undue modification.

The Flak 43 was mainly used on mobile platforms, as by 1944 it was recognised that even a Flak gun with the Flak 43's superior performance if static would itself become a target as the overwhelming number of ground attack aircraft that the allied powers operated, swarming nearly unopposed over the German areas of operation in the last years of the war in Europe. Amongst these mobile gun platforms were the last of the Sd.Kfz. 7/2s produced, the heavy weapons carrier *Schwere Wehrmachtschlepper* (sWS), and even a specially adapted version of Bussing Nag's 4.5ton 4 wheel drive truck

From its entry into production in late 1943 the Germans managed to produce 7,216 Flak 43s (note twin gun mounts were counted as two guns) and in all approximately 20,000 3.7 cm Flak guns of all type were produced from the introduction of the series.

There were a couple of other variations on the 3.7 cm Flak during its development and service life, but all were produced only in relatively small numbers. These developments included the Bordkanone BK 3.7 cm, a weapon specially designed from converted Flak 18s for mounting into aircraft designed for use in the anti-tank role. It was fitted in the Junkers Ju 87 G Stuka *Panzerknacker*, the Ju 88 P-2 and P-3 sub types, the Messerschmitt Bf 110 G and the Henschel Hs 129 B-2/R3

The other type was a variation developed from the original prototype that was intended for installation on German submarine conning towers, the infamous U-boat's "winter gardens". It was intended to protect them from marauding Sunderland flying boats and PBY Catalinas of RAF's Coastal Command, amongst other aircraft.

Modern developments of the highly successful Flak 43 weapon are still in service today with the Russian army and its previous satellite states, as well as many other Third World nations around the world supplied by the former USSR.

3.7 cm Flak 18

This 3.7 cm Flak 18 is being fired at an imaginary target. A posed photograph taken on the Baltic coast during an exercise in 1938. Of note is the soldier with the shoulder harness mount and its associated 1.2 meter range finder. Whilst this device was often used in conjunction with the Flak 18, it would not be normal to stand so close to the gun whilst it as being fired, as in order to use the instrument correctly it had to be held very steadily.

This pair of 3.7 cm Flak 18s were pictured taking part in a parade for the German public. Parades such as this were encouraged by the Nazi government to propagate their view that army was an integral part of the greater German people, an approach that they fostered throughout the pre-war period.

Below: This 3.7 cm Flak 18 is emplaced in a dug-out to lower its silhouette and also to provide a limited amount of cover from a close hit from artillery fire or a bomb. The sides of the emplacement are supported by a retaining wall made from branches woven in a wicker-style sheet to prevent the wall of the dug-out collapsing. This photo was taken in August 1940 on the perimeter of a temporary airfield in the Pas de Calais, France.

In this photograph and the one below we have a 3.7 cm Flak 18 on the parade ground of the *Luftwaffe* barracks in Leipzig, Germany. The top photo shows the weapon with its transportation bogies attached (Sd. Anh. 104) and its crew preparing to lower it on to the ground. Note the crewman about to lower the support leg from its stowed position. In the lower photo we see the same weapon but now on the ground being inspected by senior officers, this photo also shows the cruciform gun platform to good effect.

Another photograph from the same Leipzig barracks as featured on the last page; however in this picture we see the weapon being played with by the senior officers who we last saw inspecting the weapon. Of note here are the two hooks clearly visible that one of the bogies of the Sd. Anh. would latch onto before being winched into the gun's transportation configuration.

Here we see a Flak 18 being prepared to undertake firing practice on a coastal firing range on the Baltic coast near the German port of Kiel in November 1939.

A 3.7 cm Flak 18 in great detail seen here in firing configuration on a crisp winter's day during January of 1940. Note the detail of the gunner's pedestal on the gun's left-hand side and the gun's sights that are seen here fitted in place at the top of the pedestal on a swing arm that is mechanically linked to the gun's cradle so that as one elevates so does the other. Lastly it is of interest that this weapon is camouflaged not the usual monotone Panzer Grey that was the norm at this time, but with dark patches that are visible by their tonal difference.

This 3.7 cm Flak 18 is coupled up with its towing vehicle, a Krupp L3H163 off-road 4x6 truck. It is parked outside a café in Wels, Austria, only days after the German *Anschluss* (annexation) of Austria on 12th March 1938

A good close-up of a Flak 18 having just arrived at the firing range on the Baltic coast close to the port of Kiel, just outside the village of Panker. The crew are about to take the rain cover off the gun to commence setting it up for firing. Of note is the total lack of military insignia on these German *Luftwaffe* soldiers' overalls

A great view of this wooden flak tower built on the Belgian coast close to the village of Blankenberge, to the west of the Belgian port of Zeebrugge. The photo, taken in June of 1941, shows just how fast the crew of this permanent battery were setting up their life – a hut to sleep in with ablutions attached and no doubt a vegetable crop in the land between their hut and the tower.

Bottom: This timber Flak tower located somewhere on the Dutch coast shows the changes brought about by time as Allied raids began to become a more regular occurrence. The need for camouflage was attended to. Note here the netting over the crew's wooden hut, also the sighting notes marked up on plaques around the tower's inner walls, giving exact ranges to visible landmarks around the tower to aid in giving the gunner fast accurate targeting data as a potential target flew near.

This posed action photo, taken during an exercise in the fields close to the barracks in Paderborn, Germany, gives us a good indication of the crew positions in a firing scenario for this 3.7 cm Flak 18. Albeit they all look a bit too relaxed about it. Note the loader holding a six-round ammunition clip.

Another posed photo taken in roughly the same area as the last one, but of interest here is the gun being set up to fire whilst still mounted to its Sd. Anh. 104 transportation bogie system. Whilst this time-saving expedient got the gun into action quicker, the effect of the sprung bogie system on the stability of the gun must have had a large impact on the accuracy of fire.

A great group/crew portrait for the album and family back home. This is the type of shot I appreciate as it is unconcerned and natural, showing the men in an informal relaxed manner – as it would have been for the majority of the time they served here in occupied Norway.

Another natural shot of a gun crew on duty, seen here in their wicker walled gun emplacement that no doubt had soil and or sand bags piled up on the outside to give some level of ballistic protection. Note in the left rear of the photo the ready ammunition lockers also made of timber, but with some roofing felt nailed over it to give some protection for the ammunition. Note the post in the foreground that would have been used to take the weight of the barrel whilst the crew performed maintenance to the hydraulic elevation system and recoil dampers.

Whist taken at an odd angle, this interesting shot shows the weapon actually being fired. The gun barrel is captured in partial recoil, the breech is open ejecting a spent cartridge – witnessed by the puff of smoke- and also evidenced by other puffs of smoke. At least two other rounds have already been fired.

This interesting photograph is a close-up of a 3.7 cm Flak 18 being readied to fire. The gun's sight is screwed onto its mount by the crew man third from the left with the one on the far right holding its base steady. The gunner looks on intently, he is second in from the left.

This 3.7 cm Flak 18 is set up in a semi-permanent location protecting a nearby coal-fired power station near Hanover, Germany. The crew accommodation hut is seen in the background. Other photographs from this album show that this site also had at least four large 1.5 meter searchlights as well as a full battery of 3.7 cm Flak guns on strength.

A great photo of a Flak 18 set up on a raised and levelled wooden firing platform in a field outside the German city of Koblenz in the winter of 1939/40. Note here clearly visible is the elevation system's hydraulic damper cylinder (the tube attached to the circular part via an actuating arm in the foreground).

Another very clear photograph of a Flak 18, but this time from its left-hand side. Note the ready ammunition clip in its ready tray, but the gun sight is not yet fitted to the gunner's control pedestal mount. I do understand that the Flak 18 was only produced in relatively small numbers, mostly due to its cost and weight issues, but to me it is by far the best looking flak gun ever – I do hope that one day a kit becomes available for it!

A 3.7 cm Flak18 mounted to its Sd. Anh. 104 bogie system and being towed through northern France by a Henschel D33 6x4 off-road truck during the advance to take France in the summer of 1940. The crew here are being handed their bread ration from a sack on the rear of the truck. It was the weight, complexity and cost of the gun's cruciform gun platform and its associated Sd. Anh. 104 twin bogie system that brought about the gun's demise, not any lack of its effectiveness in the field.

This 3.7 cm Flak 18 is seen in the garage area that was part of the Munster Barracks complex in the summer of 1940. Unusually, many of the gun crew are pictured carrying their personal weapons whilst manhandling the flak gun.

A Flak 18 being repaired to fire in a cold snowy field, in the winter of 1940/41. Note the senior NCO using his elbow to knock the sights home in their mounting, hardly the correct tool but I guess it got the job done!

A fantastically evocative photograph of a Flak 18's firing pit dug into the valley side of the river Rhine somewhere close to the town of Bonn, Germany, in the summer of 1942, with its crew relaxing in the sun. However the gunner is still at the ready, seated in his firing position on the left-hand side of the gun.

This Flak 18 is being readied to fire; it is located in a shallow dug-out somewhere in northern Holland during the summer of 1941. Note the crew members readying the 6 round clips of ammunition for the gun. One is about to load a clip onto the feed tray while another is taking a clip from an ammunition tin that contained two full six-round clips. Note the home-made ammunition lockers, covered with lengths of carpet to protect the ammunition from the elements.

Below: A nice portrait shot of a 3.7 cm Flak 18, still with its travel lock engaged over it barrel, emplaced on the firing ranges on the Baltic coast during a pleasant summer's evening in 1939.

This close-up of a Flak 18 being fired at the Baltic coast range clearly shows an ejected spent cartridge spinning out of the open breech, still smoking as the fumes from the burnt propellant escape from the case.

A nice clear photograph of these soldiers manhandling this Flak 18 into its desired firing position, on a cold snowy day in the early winter of 1940/41 somewhere in the hills of the Norwegian wilderness. Due to the strategic nature of Norway in the supply of Germany's required iron ore, the RAF paid many visits to its coastal waters looking for ore transportation ships to sink as they hugged the coast for protection from land-based flak guns.

Another view from the Baltic firing range. In this photograph we can see three of this flak unit's weapons. It must have been a fantastic experience to witness three such weapons firing automatically so close together, the sight and sound must have been awesome.

An odd photograph from the Meppen training grounds. The guns both stand with their barrels at full elevation whilst the crew lie on the ground prone in various locations, apart from the drill instructor standing in the background. I am not sure I know what is going on here!

This photograph was taken on the banks of the Scheldt estuary just north of Antwerp, Holland, in the late summer of 1940. It shows a Flak unit using this location as a temporary test-firing range.

A high quality photograph taken in the invasion assembly area assigned to this mobile Flak unit on the afternoon before the commencement of the invasion of Poland, in the early morning hours of 1st September 1939. This unit is equipped with the 3.7 cm Flak 18 and Krupp L3H163 off-road 4x6 trucks as their prime mover.

Three members of the crew of this Flak 18, set up in a field in northern Holland during the summer of 1941, are having a laugh at the expense of the cook house that has just delivered the gun crew's main daily meal. The one soldier holds a spoon loaded with a scoop of the day's stew taken from his mess tin, whilst the others make exaggerated attempts to find the meat content. One helpfully points out a piece of meat whilst the other uses his binoculars to search the stew for evidence of any more meat.

This gun crew pose on and around their Flak 18 for an informal portrait. The photograph was taken in the motor pool garage area of the Munster Barracks complex in the late summer of 1940.

Another good quality photograph of a Flak crew posing informally for a group photograph. Note the soldier with the shoulder harness and its support frame for the 1.2 meter range finder, however the range finder is nowhere to be seen. This photo does also give us a good view of the gunner in his seat behind the control pedestal with one leg either side of it. The foot rest that can also be seen had two pads for the gunner's feet, the one on the right also functioned as the gun's trigger.

This is the cover photo here printed in full, it shows a 3.7 cm Flak 18 on sentry duty guarding a length of the Rhine river that was navigable from the sea and for many miles inland. It was a major supply route for German industry and as such needed to be protected from Allied air strikes.

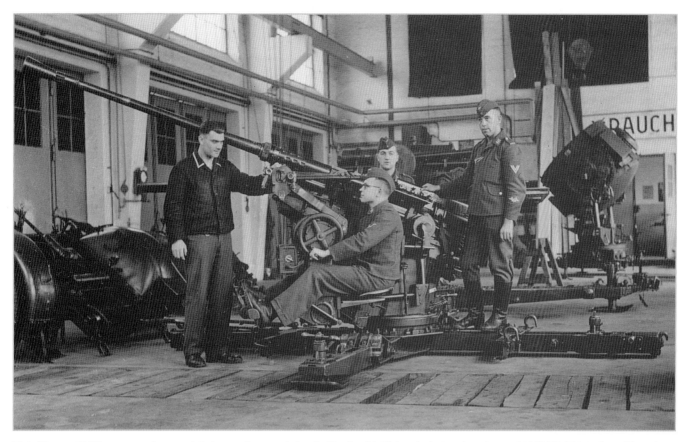

This "Panzer Hall" motor pool garage is being used as a training facility by this Flak unit during the winter of 1939/40. This informal bunch are actually a group of instructors posing for a private photograph. As well as the 3.7 cm Flak 18 seen centrally, in this photo we have one half of the Sd. Anh. 104 transport bogie system resting against the door and, in the background, a German standard 1.5 meter searchlight.

This is a good photo that gives an impression of the crew manhandling the Sd. Anh. 104 bogie elements away from the cruciform base of the Flak 18 in order to set it up in firing mode. In this case the crew are practising this procedure on the grass boundary area of Frankfurt airfield, on 21st September 1938.

Here we see another 3.7 cm Flak 18 dug into the banks of the river Rhine, there were Flak position the full length of the Rhine through- out Germany. These semi-permanent firing positions saw the Flak 18 in use to the very end of its service life. Indeed some of the very last guns in service were in these non-front line installations right up until 1945.

This Flak gun is mounted on top of a Flak tower close to the Baltic coast. Note the virtual white-out caused by the light reflecting off the snow.

This newly-constructed Flak position, made from a wicker fence as a backing wall that soil has been piled up against, will later be turfed or grass will grow on it naturally to prevent soil slippage. This particular Flak installation is on the perimeter of a radar site in northern France, close to the city of Caen.

A recently emplaced Flak 18 is having the final touches added prior to it being fully ready to fire. The location is the edge of a recently harvested section of a corn field in the Ukraine. Note the sentry securing the perimeter in the background. The photo was taken in the high summer of 1941 in the early stages of Operation Barbarossa.

Another brand-new Flak emplacement as can be seen from the newly cut and clean timber. Of interest here is the well in the background and the signal paddle hung on the wall at the left of the photo. Lastly, this crew member's portrait gives us a very good look at the gun sight fitted to its mounting arm.

Another type of flak position, here the protective bund is formed by two parallel wooden walls that have had the space between them filled with soil. The close-up view of the right-hand side of the Flak 18 affords us a very clear look at the balancing hydraulic cylinder and its actuating mechanism.

The same Flak 18 as pictured above but from a slightly higher angle. We have a good view of the breech and its spent shell ejection system. The small rectangular box fixed to the gun mount at the bottom of the photograph was to stow the gun sight in during transit, to keep it both clean and safe. Also of note are the two different styles of ammunition box stowed in the small recessed hole in the bund's wall.

Opposite page bottom: Here we have yet another form of flak position, this one is surrounded by multiple layers of coal sacks filled with soil. I may be being fooled by perspective but this Flak position looks to be slightly raised and blocking the track it appears to be mounted on. The 3.7 cm Flak 18's crew is of most interest here – looking at their uniforms, the three on the right are wearing the usual *Luftwaffe* field uniforms while the three on the left of the photo are wear- ing black work overalls.

This 3.7 cm Flak 18, that has obviously been emplaced for some time – note the well-trodden down vegetation surrounding the weapon – is about to be moved onto another firing position. The first of the two halves of the Sd. Anh. 104 transportation bogies are being hooked up to the gun's cruciform base by the crew, the other is obviously out of shot currently.

This is wonderful portrait of the gunner of this Flak 18. The gun is in an open firing position and it is set up to guard the fresh water reservoir that serves the town of Cloppenburg in northern Germany. Of note is the use of wooden duckboards on the soft ground to be walked on and the concrete paving slab that has been used as a foundation base block for one of the gun's cruciform base levelling pads.

This photo is of the same Flak 18 emplacement as seen on page 28, but here the gun's crew are present on this spring afternoon, 24th April 1941. Of note is the age of the crew. As the war progressed the crews would get younger as the original crew were transferred to combat units, in some cases even female *Luftwaffe* auxiliaries performed some of the duties in operating an em- placed Flak gun behind the front lines protecting a strategic location.

Left: At first sight this looks like an odd set up, with the Flak control system and associated optical sighting equipment located on a raised platform while the |flak gun is set up to fire on the ground close by. In fact this is a firing range and the tower here is for the use of the instructors and inspect- ing officers.

3.7 cm Flak 36

The crew of this 3.7 cm Flak 36 are pictured at an informal moment and having a laugh together. The life of a Flak crew was made up of many hours of watching and waiting, intersected by moments of intense activity and danger. This gun has only just been set up, as witnessed by the complete lack of any form of protective enclosure or gun pit, and the Sd. Anh. bogies can still be seen in the background. The photograph was taken on the French coast close to Le Havre in June 1940.

A nice close-up of a 3.7 cm Flak 36 set up on the perimeter of a temporary air strip on the Russian steppe during the campaign of the summer of 1942. In the background is the farm house that the crew are using as accommodation. I doubt that the previous occupants are still around to protest. Clearly visible in the photo are both the electrical cable to conduct power to the sights and the cord that is attached to the cocking handle so that the gun can be cocked more easily. The cocking handle was a short rod and it took a lot of effort to pull fully back to cock this large 3.7 cm gun. A rope attached to the rod was a good idea.

An interesting close-up of a Flak 36's left-hand side, showing to good effect the loader's seat and the chain attaching the folding seat to the folding floor panel below so that as you fold the seat the floor panel would fold up as well. Of note in this photo of a Flak installation in the Sangatte area of northern France is that both the visible ammunition clips are loaded with just the one sort of ammunition. This is the HET round. Whist many different types of ammunition became available for the 3.7 cm German flak guns, there were three common types available, the HE (high explosive), AP (armour piercing) and HET (high explosive with tracer).

This 3.7 cm Flak 36 is in its protective dugout that has log work retaining walls. The firing position was photographed in the summer of 1942, just east of Calais, France. Note that all eight members of the flak crew are in the photo, so someone else must have been on hand to take the pic. Lastly, note the crew member with the 1.2 meter range finder that it is still attached to the shoulder harness but is in the forward rest position.

Below: Another 3.7 cm Flak 36 gun position in northern France, this one is very well established and the recently harvested wheat straw adds to the effectiveness of its camouflage. Of interest is the wooden box in the foreground – it would normally contain the cleaning kit and pull through and patch cloth for the gun, but all has been removed and yet no cleaning seems to be being carried out?

In order to prevent the Allies from being able to plot a safe route through Germany's Flak defences on the Dutch, Belgian and French coast, they not only had fixed Flak positions protecting potential targets they also used mobile Flak units that would move from location to location sometime every two or three days, so that no route could be considered as safe. This mobile 3.7 cm Flak 36 is set up in a recently harvested field close to the Belgian village of Roeselare in the high summer of 1943.

This 3.7 cm Flak 36 is part of the *Luftwaffe* troop's defensive armament on the island of Sicily, close to the town of Gela, not far from the very beaches the Allied invasion forces would eventually arrive at on 9th July 1943. This gun crew are certainly expecting to be in action, look at the piles of ready ammunition clips, each containing six 3.7 cm rounds, lying open close to the gun.

This rare action photograph was also taken in Sicily on 10th July, just one day after the Allies have landed. This particular gun was set up in the hills above the capital city of Palermo, that is seen burning just the other side of the hill in the background.

Opposite page bottom:
The *Luftwaffe* crew of this Flak 36 are posing proudly for an informal group photo it was taken on an airfield in Belgium, but sadly I do not know which one. The use of corrugated tin for the emplacements retaining walls is interesting as this rare resource was usually kept for roofing in WWII unlike in WWI when there seemed to be an unlimited supply of the stuff and it appeared nearly everywhere. Metal was more precious in the 1940's as more war equipment needed it, unlike in earlier times when wood was still the major component in most items.

A nice photograph of a line-up of 3.7 cm Flak 36s ready for inspection on the parade ground of the *Luftwaffe* field regiment's barracks in Luneburg. Taken in the summer of 1939 this photograph shows the Flak guns mounted in their transport trailers, the Sd. Anh. 52.

This photograph was taken on the same parade ground early one morning in the autumn of 1939. The soldiers are up early setting up their equipment for an inspection to be held later in the day. I have to say that this type of BS was the one side of military life that I just found ridiculous and a total waste of my time and training.

A snowy day in January 1943 sees this Flak 36 and its crew on duty on the hills above an industrial area on the outskirts of the German town of Glessen. Ready ammunition is spread all over the place as are empty ammunition boxes, an indication that this crew have had a busy night thanks to the RAF.

Below: This Flak installation is dug into a garden of a residential house (of a very modern design) in the Weser Valley to the south-east of the German city of Bremen. It is an odd location as it does not offer a 360° field of fire, the house will surely prove an obstacle to both observing a low flying enemy and indeed engaging it with fire. The site must be considered semi-permanent as a lot of work has gone into the ground work around the firing platform, turf has even been used to give more support to the earthwork embankment.

A real candid view of military life – after a long night on duty these two gun crew have had their breakfast and are catching a quick nap while they can. Note the mess tin on the gunner's seat and the lump of black bread also left unfinished. I can attest that sleep is one of the rarest commodities in combat, and any and all opportunities to sleep were taken.

A typical day in the life of a Flak crew. A nice relaxed group portrait of the gun crew of this 3.7 cm Flak 36, who are on duty giving watch over the perimeter of the Peenemünde weapons research facility close to the German/Polish border on the Baltic coast. Of note is the observation that the only member of the crew who is wearing his greatcoat is the seated gunner, as he will be the most inactive and therefore will get cold the quickest – and a cold gunner is a slow and inaccurate gunner, even his hands are tucked into his pockets.

Right: A busy scene as this flak unit based in Paderborn, Germany in 1939 prepares for a day on the firing range. It is of note that here there are no Panzer halls for the storage of the weapons but merely a Dutch barn (any barn with a roof but no walls) type arrangement. Of note is the very light colour of the uniforms the troops are all wearing. This is the white twill M1933 fatigue uniform, issued to all troops for use for labouring tasks, and when not in the field.

Opposite page bottom: This photo, taken somewhere on the coast of Denmark, gives us a good look at the top of the 3.7 cmFlak 36. We can see the top of the gun sight at the right bottom of the photo, then the cocking spring housing on top of the gun's breech and lastly the ammunition feed tray, here loaded with a full clip of six HE Flak rounds. Note the sixth round is already loaded in the weapon's breech.

The gun crew are captured here performing the daily maintenance required to keep the Flak 36 at the peak of its performance. The standing soldier in the foreground is holding the cleaning rod that was made up of three sections that screwed together. Note the used cotton cleaning patch is still partially attached to its end. Also note the crew member at the far left of the picture. He is re-attaching the flash suppressor to the end of the barrel with its special tool; and lastly note the open long open timber box in the foreground behind the crew's gas masks and helmets. It is a spares box that contains two new barrels as well as the disassembled cleaning rod, a box of cotton patches and the wire brush attachment that could be fitted to the top of the cleaning rod to scour the barrel's rifling when it became badly clogged up with carbon residue.

This Flak 36 has been set up to watchover the entrance to the Belgian port of Oostende, next to part of the old Napoleonic defence complex. The photo was taken during the height of the evacuation of the BEF from Dunkirk that was taking place only a few miles west of this location at the time.

This action photo was taken in the late Russian summer of 1941, and shows the nonchalance of combat that befalls some solders especially when in a group as company inspires confidence and a false sense of safety. The bridge this Flak 36 has been tasked with protecting has come under artillery fire and a number of hits have started fires along its length, the Flak crew can do nothing to prevent this and are just standing as spectators while the bridge is pounded by the barrage.

Below: An enigmatic portrait of a 3.7 cm Flak 36's crew member watching the horizon through his binoculars. This gun's firing position is protected by an emplacement made from sand bags and is located on a farm in the southern part of Greece. What makes this position of more interest is that the emplacement was built by the British only days before and was abandoned when they retreated and were eventually evacuated from Greece to Crete, during the period of 24th April to 1st May 1941.

This photograph shows a 3.7 cm Flak 36 and its raised gun platform, made from timber walls with a soil infill. It is set up to protect the valuable coal and iron ore barges that are using the Gent-Bruges canal. At the time the photo was taken in the winter of 1940/42 the crew are undergoing a gas attack drill. These drills became less and less common as the war progressed, as no use of gas was reported – to the extent that even gas mask containers themselves became a rare sight to see on a German soldier in the later stages of the war.

Below: In Holland in 1943, we see a flood plain where the Germans have released the water from the dykes to produce an area of flooding. This was in order to make any potential invasion by the Allies an impossible task or at least very costly in manpower. I like this picture of a relaxed crew eating their lunch whilst on duty in the field, as it demonstrates to me that in the midst of war, normal life has to go on.

A very high quality photograph of a group of officers during an inspection of an emplaced 3.7 cm Flak 36. The photo shows a number of interesting features, including the padded mat fixed to the front of the armour plate over the gunner's position where spent cases are ejected and could hit the armour. Note that a screwdriver has been slipped down behind the mat for safe-keeping and ease of access. It was obviously a tool that was in regular use, otherwise it would have been replaced in the weapon's tool kit. This photograph was taken on 16th May 1943 at a permanent Flak installation on the perimeter of an airfield located at Carpiquet near Caen, France.

A good photograph of a 3.7 cm Flak 36 gun crew preparing their weapon for action. Seen here on the hills overlooking the port of Odessa in the summer of 1942 in what looks to be a nicely set up gun position and associated accommodation.

A 3.7 cm Flak 36 in a new Flak position that is being set up in Norway. Note the pegs in the ground arranged around the gun position, they will be markers illustrating landmarks visible from the gun's position and will provide the gunner with accurate distances to those landmarks, in order for the gunner to better aim at a target flying over any one of them. Note the open ammunition box with one of the six-round clips half way removed and the spare barrel box on the far right of the photo.

Another good photo of a 3.7 cm Flak 36. Interestingly, some of the crew are in civilian clothes ready for a night out, but of more interest here is the recognisable location. Any of our British readers who have been on a trip to Le Havre, France, has probably walked over this location as it is where, in the 1970s, a huge hypermarket and shopping complex was constructed. But the same skyline can still be viewed from the car park.

This photograph was taken just outside a railway marshalling yard in northern Serbia in the spring of 1943. If this photo was posed it has been done well, as the observers and the gunner all look to watching exactly the same spot in the sky. The gun position is just a shallow pit with the dug up earth piled up around its edge adding to the protection for the gun and crew. Of note here is the field telephone line laid on the ground and then protected by what looks to be lengths of cut timber boarding lying on top of it.

Just one soldier is on sentry duty at this 3.7 cm Flak 36 installation, that has been set up in dug out gun pits that have lined with wooden plank retaining walls. The wood has been painted as well, a certain sign that the Flak gun was there to stay. The crew accommodation hut and outdoor lavatory hut are both visible in this photo as is the industrial area in the background that the weapon is here to protect.

This low quality photograph has been included as I think it is of interest, it shows both the standard 3.7 cm Flak 36 that used the Sd. Anh. 52 trailer for its transportation and a Flak 36 that is the armament attached to the weapons platform at the rear of an Sd.Kfz. 6/1. The 3.7 cm Flak saw service on many mobile platforms but the most common were the Büssing-NAG 4.5 ton truck, the Sd.Kfz. 6/1, the Sd.Kfz. 7/2 and the Panzer IV Ostwind, amongst many other field conversions or factory prototypes.

Opposite page, bottom: Here we see a 3.7 cm Flak 36 set up on the cliffs above the English Channel just to the north-east of the French coastal town of Saint-Valery-en-Caux, the same town that the remnants of the BEF fought their final action in, having covered the evacuation of their comrades from the beaches of Dunkirk. This last stand took place in mid-June of 1940, this photo was taken in August of that same year. The photo gives us a very good view of the elongated triangular baseplate that replaced the cruciform of the earlier Flak 18.

At the roadside this 3.7 cm Flak 36 has been set up to cover a route that has been taken regularly by low-flying intruders in recent days. The the crew of this mobile Flak unit have set the trap and as soon as the aircraft comes over the ridge they will engage it with a hail of 3.7 cm fire. Traps such as this work very well against low-flying aircraft and the Allies suffered losses to such traps. This photo was taken in northern Germany on 14th May 1943.

This 3.7 cm Flak 36 has been set up on beach on the North Sea Coast somewhere on the island of Sylt. The *Luftwaffe* had one of their main weapons-testing airfields based on the island, and it was well defended. Of note in this photo is yet another form of ammunition box. Note the crew hanging a poncho over the breech and recoil runners on the gun's cradle in an attempt to keep as much sand off these sensitive lubricated areas as possible. Sand and guns are not a good mix.

Bottom: This mobile Flak battery has set up their 3.7 cm Flak 36 to fire from a recently harvested wheat field in northern Belgium in the high summer of 1943. In this view we get a good close-up look at the spare barrel box and some of the special tools.

In this photograph we see a recent upgrade to a defensive position located on the Hook of Holland. This 3.7 cm Flak 36 has just been installed in a well-prepared emplacement that, up until the 3.7 cm gun's arrival, was the home to a 20 mm Flak 38 that has been taken away by another of the Demag D7s (Sd.Kfz. 10s) that we see in the background.

Below: Here we have another 3.7 cm Flak 36 in a very well made gun emplacement. Whilst not a concrete emplacement, this wooden one give a very good impression of a field made semi-permanent fixture. Its layout is very well done, including the lockers built into the walls for both ammunition and associated equipment required by the weapon. Note the brand new cocking rope lanyards that were used to cock the weapon hung over the gunner's armour plate. In fact the whole gun looks to be in as new condition, its Panzer Grey paint looks brand new yet this photo dates from 1943, the year when German standard factory finish paint colour was changed from Panzer Grey to overall Dark Yellow. This this may well be one of the last guns to have received this earlier colour paint.

A 3.7 cm Flak 36 that has just been dropped off from its Sd. Anh. 52 transport trailer and is being set up on the hills above the city of Montenegro, Yugoslavia. (Now Podgorica, the capital city of Montenegro and, after the war until 1992, Titogrado). Note the crew member with the shovel – he is about to start to dig a trench around the gun position and pile up the spoil to form a protective bund. This gun is protecting one of the routes that Allied aircraft regularly took from Italy to attack the Ploesti oil fields in Romania.

Here we see a 3.7 cm Flak 36 being fired at a range located on the Baltic coast by a group of officers, whilst the gun's usual crew help out by doing all the loading, fetching and carrying. Of interest in this photo is the small white lettering spelling the word "braun" on the gun cradle. This refers to the type of oil to be used in the recoil cylinders. Two types were available, "braun" an oil for temperate climates and "ark" an oil for very cold or winter climates. As the war progressed this choice was done away with by the replacement of the two separate oils with a mix of both that could be used in all weathers. The stencilling would then read "braun/ark" and is found on many artillery pieces from late 1942 onwards.

In a French wheat field the crew of this mobile 3.7 cm Flak gun have set up a temporary home. The gun is at the ready with one crew member standing watch whilst two others are playing a board game next to the gun. Their tent made from their combined ponchos and other personal items, that include a box full of eggs, are seen on the right of the photo.

This well set up flak position is one of many that by 1944 would have been replaced by a permanent concrete gun emplacement. The position protects the area just north of the Hook of Holland and as such was eventually an important part of the Atlantic Wall fortifications. Here in the early spring of 1941 it was still a timber-lined dug-out type of emplacement.

This high quality close-up of a 3.7 cm Flak 36 mounted to its transportation trailer, the Sd. Anh. 52, offers us a great view of how the loader's seat and platform floor folded up so the that gun could fit the narrow trailer. Like nearly all other military equipment of the day, one of the first design criteria of any and all equipment was to ensure that it would fit the standard width European railway gauge.

An emplaced *Luftwaffe* 3.7 cm Flak 36 in the fields behind the village of Sangatte, France, close to Calais, where the Germans were building a pair of very large bunkers for a two-gun battery of K5e railway guns to operate from. Once the K5e bunkers were completed no doubt permanent bunkers were then made for their protective flak installations, but they would have been manned by army personnel and the mobile *Luftwaffe* unit reassigned.

Atop a Flak tower in the German industrial city of Duisburg, that by 1944 had three of them to protect some strategic factories located there, such as Demag and Siemens. The town boasted an inland port on the navigable part of the river Rhine. This photo gives us a good look at the left-hand side of the 3.7 cm Flak 36 in its firing position, note here the two spare six-round clips stacked on the loader's floor panel and another of Duisburg's Flak towers in the far background. The pointed style tower also in the background is part of one of the town's ornate bridges that sadly did not survive the war.

Note: one of Duisburg's Flak towers is still intact today and as far as I know is the last of its kind still around. It is now home of the local rock climbing club, who use the modified outside walls for practice climbs with varying degrees of difficulty on each of its four sides.

Opposite page, bottom: An interesting photograph this, here we see the ex-French army barracks in Sedan that have been taken over by the occupying German forces. However the effects of the German bombing of the barracks is still evident and many building repairs are to be seen still to be carried out. On the parade ground outside the main barracks are a 20 mm Flak 30 mounted on its Sd. Anh. 51 trailer and a 3.7 cm Flak 36 mounted on its Sd. Anh. 52 trailer respectively. Also seen are three Kar98 rifles in a pyramid stack, all ready for an inspection.

A very good photograph of this 3.7 cm Flak 36 that was only ever meant to be an informal group portrait for the crew to be able to keep or send home. However it actually offers us an excellent clear view of the elevation gear of the flak gun and the lower elements of the gun cradle.

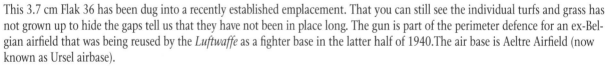

This 3.7 cm Flak 36 has been dug into a recently established emplacement. That you can still see the individual turfs and grass has not grown up to hide the gaps tell us that they have not been in place long. The gun is part of the perimeter defence for an ex-Belgian airfield that was being reused by the *Luftwaffe* as a fighter base in the latter half of 1940. The air base is Aeltre Airfield (now known as Ursel airbase).

A 3.7 cm Flak 36 anti-aircraft gun emplaced somewhere in the Ukraine in the early winter of 1942/43. The crew seem to have jumped the gun a bit with the overall white winter camouflage paint job on the gun shield, it kind of stands out against the mud that that is covering everything else in sight. It is noteworthy that this crew portrait does not show the crew smiling or making a show of being happy for the camera – they all look rather pensive, if not worried about what the coming Russian winter will have in store for them.

Below: This group of officers are inspecting a 3.7 cm Flak 36 in the grounds of the barracks in Koblenz, Germany, in 1939. It is brand new and probably has only just been issued to this unit and that's why the officers are giving this weapon the once over. Note the non-standard gunner's shield, a discarded prototype probably, but it has not been wasted.

A great study of a flak crew and their charge, this photograph was taken in Leipzig, Germany, in 1938. Whilst the gun is as always the centre of attention I can't help but notice that two of the soldiers are smoking whilst on duty – obviously the rules on smoking on duty were very different then. I also see the unusual placement of two full six-round ammunition clips on the lower plate of the gunner's protective shield, odd as they load from the other side.

This Flak 36 is firing at a drone target. The Germans pioneered the use of radio-controlled aircraft as drones and whilst due to cost they were not in common use, when they were used they drew a crowd just as you see here. Also of note is the amount of ammunition that has been withdrawn from the armoury for this target practice.

We have seen this 3.7 cm Flak 36 before on the same range firing at a radio-controlled aircraft drone, this close up gives us a very clear view of the right-hand side of the gun and the gun's cocking handle is very evident. Due to the strength required to pull the bolt back to cock the weapon, a rope lanyard was often used. Also note the white number "2" painted on the barrel support, it is the gun's number within the battery.

Below: The same gun as above, as witnessed by the "No 2" painted on the mudguard of the Sd. Anh. 52 trailer. I have included this photo as, whilst the gun is completely hidden, it does offer a very good view of the factory supplied weather cover for transport. An item rarely photographed as it's not interesting to many, but it was in regular use and a common sight.

This 3.7 cm Flak 36 is positioned in a well-constructed emplacement, a dug-out with timber retaining walls and a covered ammunition locker. This unmanned weapon is also missing the gun sight, so I can only surmise that it is either about to undergo maintenance or has just been maintained and awaits the crew to put the final touches in place, such as load it with ammo and refit the sight. This view however does give us another good look at the left-hand side of the weapon.

This is a relatively new gun position as can be seen by the recent application of turf to the emplacement's walls to bind the soil together. This gun is part of the Flak battery assigned to protect the area around the French town of Livarot, where Rommel was taken when he was injured by an attack on his staff car by an RAF Typhoon on 17 July 1944.

This photograph of a 3.7 cm Flak 36 and its crew are shown here at action stations searching the sky for potential targets. This weapon from a mobile Flak unit is set up in the open to protect a length of railway line. By 1943 the Allied tactic of using railway lines as both navigation aids and targets of opportunity was well known and so it became necessary for mobile flak units to be given different lengths of railway line to protect on a regular basis. The flak guns would be moved from site to site so that no effective counter-attack could be made against them. It is a relatively little known fact that the biggest toll of flak guns destroyed in service was not achieved by the attacking Allied ground forces, but from the Allies' overwhelming superiority of ground attack aircraft in numbers, quality and effectiveness.

This photo from the autumn of 1944 shows the crew of this 3.7 cm Flak 36 to be made up of mostly older men than we have seen up until now. As the war progressed, more and more of the original flak crew were transferred to the front for infantry duty and their tasks were taken up by men too old or unfit for normal military duty. Here we see a motley group of men in all types of clothing, bits of military uniform mixed with civilian clothing. Only the gunner, loader and gun commander look to be from the original flak crew.

This 3.7 cm Flak 36 emplacement is obviously well established. The wood retaining walls look to have some age to them and the crew have had plenty of time to make up range marker plaques and nail them to the relevant points around the emplacement, to give aid to the gunner in estimating the correct range whilst engaging a target. This photo of one of the crew gives us a clear view of the left-hand rear of the weapon and in the foreground the handle of the rear levelling pad jack.

Both this and the photo below are of a 3.7 cm Flak 36 anti-aircraft gun and its crew that have been assigned to protect the Heinkel factory known as Heinkel-Nord (Heinkel-North), that was built in the Rostock-Marienehe area (today known as Rostock-Schmarl) along the west bank of the Unterwarnow estuary. The gun appears to be brand new and has probably only just been issued to this unit, who will in time locate the weapon into an emplacement somewhere close by. The photo was taken on 4th April 1940.

Here we see a flak unit based at Meppen undergoing an inspection, but this is just the pre-inspection inspection carried out by senior NCOs to ensure that all is in good order to be inspected by officers later that day – such a waste of time! Of interest in this photo is the is the ammunition box fixed to the rear of the tool locker on the mudguard of the Sd. Anh. 52. It is a very small one, it would have only held one six-round clip. The standard ammunition box in this style was made to carry two clips of ammo. Also note the clear view of the padlock on the tool locker. It is of the standard type seen on all kinds of military equipment and vehicle tool lockers throughout the war.

Below: This 3.7 cm Flak 36 is in its emplacement next to the Kiel Canal, close to the town of Brunsbuttle on the River Elbe. This major shipping route was well protected throughout the war and was also a regular target for the Allied air forces. Of note is the amount of ready to use ammunition piled up in the tray on the loader's floor plate, and lastly it looks like one of the crew has brought his son to work!

This well-established 3.7 cm Flak 36 emplacement is in the Dutch countryside during the summer of 1942. This crew are expecting action – the pile of ready ammunition attests to that. The loader is holding a six-round clip and give us a very good view of it. Noteworthy is that all the ammunition in the clips is of the anti-aircraft type but not the type fitted with a tracer pellet in the projectile's base.

This 3.7 cm Flak 36 is mounted on top of a Flak tower. Unfortunately I have no clue as to where it was as no inscription is on the album or the rear of the photo. However it is a nice shot of the weapon's loader holding a six-round clip of standard anti-aircraft rounds. Of note is the rope lanyard hung over the rear of the gun, this was used to assist in cocking the weapon, a task possible to do by pulling on the handle directly but much easier with two hands pulling on the rope when attached to the cocking handle.

Another well-established gun emplacement in which we find a combat ready 3.7 cm Flak 36 and one member of its crew standing on watch. In this picture we have a great example of the way that ranging plaques were used, as we can clearly see the range plaque on the far wall of the emplacement stating that a tower that is illustrated on the plaque is 1,220 meters away and above the wall in the far distance we can actually the tower the plaque refers to.

This photo is of the same gun as above but here we have eight of the crew members in an informally posed group portrait. This photo was taken in the high summer of 1942 somewhere inland of the Belgian port of Ostend.

A 3.7 cm Flak 36 that is part of a mobile Flak unit that moves from site to site, usually only staying in one location from between 3 to 10 days. This gun is combat ready under its protective tarpaulin, the stack of ready to use six-round clips can be seen on the loader's platform floor. The gun's associated Sd. Anh. 52 trailer is in the background, to the left of the assembled gun crew who are waiting on food to be delivered. The weapon is set up in the fields close to the Dutch industrial town of Hengelo, that was on the main line railway network as well as being located by the side of the Twentekanaal waterway.

This flak battery is set up on the rocky slope that leads to part of the river Loire's estuary, close to the U-Boat docks at St-Nazaire. They have set up away from the port to undertake some target practice. Of interest here is the officer with binoculars, the NCO with a 1.2 metre range finder out of its tube and being held at rest on his right-hand side and lastly, another officer with a writing board on which he is no doubt keeping records of the accuracy, efficiency and discipline of the various guns and guns crews within the Flak unit.

A member of the 3.7 cm Flak 36 crew sits on watch whilst using the time to clean his personal weapon, a Kar98 7.92 mm Mauser rifle. This Flak gun has been emplaced in the hills above a village to the east of Esbjerg, close to the North Sea coast. The gun is in place not only to protect the town and the railway line in the valley below, but also no doubt the Freya radar installation that can just be seen in the far distance.

A good group portrait of the crew of this 3.7 cm Flak 36, in a field somewhere in Italy in late September of 1943, only weeks after the Italians surrendered to the Allies on the 8th of that month.

Tun antiaerian Rheinmetall calibru 37 mm model 1939

The Flak 36/37 became the most numerous variant of the 3.7 cm anti-aircraft gun and this was partly due to it also being produced under licence in Romania by the Astra Company of Brasov. It was known in Romanian service as the Tun antiaerian Rheinmetall calibre 3.7 cm model 1939 and was manufactured at the low rate of only 10 per month, and this num- ber fell as the war progressed. The two photographed here show the differences between the Romanian version of the gun and the standard original German production, whilst the actual weapon was almost exactly the same, the gun carriage was very different. The gun's base plate was still triangular but very different in detail, but the major difference was the trailer to render the weapon mobile. Whilst the Germans used the Kfz. 52 that was for motorised transport, the Romanian design could be towed by a truck but was primarily designed for horse power traction by at least two horses but could fit four into its rig if available or required. Lastly as you can see it came with an ammunition limber to complete its ensemble.

3.7 cm Flak 37

This 3.7 cm Flak 37 mounted on to a flak tower in Wilhelmshaven has probably come from one of the German navy's scrapped ships, as Hitler had ordered many of the navy's surface ships scrapped to reuse the steel. Such was his disdain for the surface navy following the loss of the *Bismarck*, only the submarine arm of the *Kriegsmarine* was held any respect by Hitler. The weapon has no triangular ground base, as can be seen its mounting ring that would have been bolted to a ship's deck is now mounted on a pile of wooden spacers to achieve the gun's required level within the flak tower.

A 3.7 cm Flak 37 in an emplacement dugout in a field on the outskirts of the industrial town of Frankenthal, Germany. Note the main identifying feature of the Flak 37 – the barrel jacket was unperforated unlike the Flak 36 that has perforations down to the level of the recoil spring retaining bolt housing.

Below: The crew of this 3.7 cm Flak 37 have had to build a wooden platform for their weapon to be mounted on, and smaller wooden platforms for the gun's ancillaries such as the spare barrel, box and ammunition boxes, due to the soft ground they have been ordered to site their are weapon on. This location is on a river estuary that has a refinery on the opposite bank. Note the open spares box that also held the barrel's cleaning rods and that the crew are using them in this photo.

A very good close-up of the new electric sight fitted to Flak 37 and retrofitted to some Flak 36s. Also note the anti-glare coating that is now painted onto the gunner's armoured shield. Lastly we see the barrel removal special tool (a large thin spanner) mounted to the gun shield for speed of acquisition during a fast barrel change.

Another view of the same Flak 37 that shows it photographed from the same position only with the camera pointed slightly lower down. Note this late pro- duction weapon is painted overall Dark Yellow from the factory, meaning it was manufactured in late 1943 or 1944. It has been removed from its normal base, that enabled it to be hooked up to the Sd. Anh. 52 for mobility, and has been permanently mounted to the floor of the flak position on the perimeter of the *Luftwaffe* airfield at Frankfurt-Main.

Here we have more photographs of the same weapon in the same emplacement. In this good quality photograph we can see the left-hand front of this 3.7 cm Flak 37, of note is the integral ammunition box mounted on the loader's floor plate and the rope lanyard hung over the back of the gun that would have been used for cocking the weapon.

The same gun, here viewed from directly head on with a good view of the twin hydraulic elevation rams.

This 3.7 cm Flak 37 is set up outside the crew's accommodation hut located on the tree line of the perimeter of an airfield. This is a late war set up such that the trees protect the rear of the weapon from marauding ground attack aircraft and yet the gun can still fire on any target that tries to attack the airfield. While this reduced the radius of attack that the gun from almost certain destruction from one of the very aircraft it was there to defend against.

An Sd.Kfz. 7/2 half-track that the crew are working on. The gunner of this 3.7 cm Flak 37 however remains in his position, so that should a target come into range he will be ready. Note the spare barrel box placed at the rear of the gun platform, and the crew's seats folded away behind the driver's cab rear bulkhead. Also the wet weather cover is being used as a sun shade by the driver, as it certainly does not look like rain on this sunny day in Italy in 1944.

This 3.7 cm Flak 37 is located in grounds of a large country manor house near the German town of Damme in Lower Saxony, that was used as a training centre for German Army officers. This Flak gun was no doubt a major part of the centre's defences.

A 3.7 cm Flak 37 that was part of a mobile Flak unit set up in a field next to a major railway line, the gun crew are in the process of digging a bund to act as a protective wall for the crew during action. The gun would be emplaced here for 3 to 10 days in the hope of catching an Allied aircraft flying low to attack a train – flying low and straight was easy meat to a Flak 37.

This *Luftwaffe* crewed 3.7 cm Flak 36 is permanently emplaced on the perimeter of a German airfield in northern France and is photographed here in the summer of 1943. This informally posed crew portrait shows the gun off to good affect and also illustrates the crew's positions during firing very well.

Another 3.7 cm Flak 37 emplaced on an airfield perimeter to protect what was left of the *Luftwaffe* in late 1944. Note the age of the crew – the gun is being manned by children other than the gunner, and he looks no more than 18 or 19. But he must be good at his job as witnessed by the impressive number of kill rings painted on the barrel of this 3.7 cm weapon.

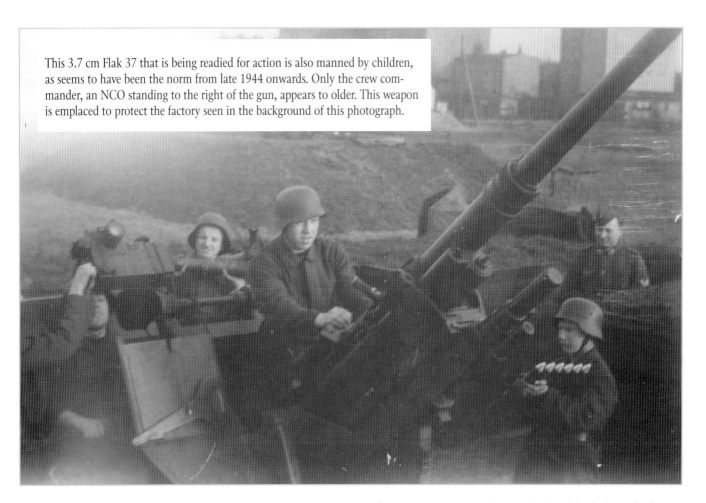

This 3.7 cm Flak 37 that is being readied for action is also manned by children, as seems to have been the norm from late 1944 onwards. Only the crew commander, an NCO standing to the right of the gun, appears to older. This weapon is emplaced to protect the factory seen in the background of this photograph.

A very atmospheric photograph of a 3.7 cm Flak 37 and its crew seen here on Christmas Day 1943 in a dug-out of reduced depth due to the frozen ground. The gun is set up to defend a nearby airstrip somewhere in the north of Russia, close to Leningrad (now St Petersburg). The weapon is obviously no stranger to combat – note the pile of ready ammunition on the loader's platform and also of interest is that the crew, all but one, are wearing the double-sided combat jacket with the white side outermost, but they are all still wearing their Field Grey forage caps.

This 3.7 cm Flak 37 is newly emplaced on the perimeter of the runway at Brandenburg-Briest airfield, west of Berlin. JV44 have just moved in and this elite unit required more Flak protection to ensure that their extremely valuable aircraft and pilots were protected in their most vulnerable moments. For a Me 262 this was during either its take-off or landing, as both took longer than in a normal piston powered aircraft as early jet engines did not power up or down with speed and if rushed the engines would flame-out. The Allies grew to know this and tried to catch them whist taking off or landing so circled the airfield, hence the requirement for extra Flak. This crew are also wearing their reversible double-sided combat jackets but here with the camouflaged side outermost.